Cultivating Communities Series

Book Two

The Virtue of Dialogue

Becoming a Thriving Church through Conversation

Revised and Updated Edition

by C. Christopher Smith

ENGLEWOODPRESS.COM

Copyright © 2025 by C. Christopher Smith
2nd edition

Published by Englewood Press
57 N. Rural Street
Indianapolis, IN 46201

www.englewoodpress.com

All rights reserved.

No portion of this book may be reproduced in any form without written permission from the publisher or author, except as permitted by U.S. copyright law.

ISBN 978-1-934406-19-9 (print)
ISBN 978-1-934406-20-5 (digital)

Library of Congress Control Number: 2025930732

Unless otherwise noted, Scripture quotations contained herein are from the *New Revised Standard Version Updated Edition,* Copyright © 2021, by the Division of Christian Education of the National Council of Churches in the United States of America.

Cover design: Eliza Whyman

Contents

The Cultivating Communities Series	VII
Preface	1
Introduction	7
1. The Rise and Fall of an Urban Mega-Church: Setting the Stage for Conversation	15
2. Becoming Rooted Together: Our Sunday Night Conversation	25
3. Becoming a Conversational People: Talking Together Throughout the Week	39
4. A Space for All to be Heard: The Hospitality of Conversation	53
5. The Virtue of Dialogue (Or, Why Conversation is an Essential Practice of Church Communities)	63

Appendix A: Questions to Engage in Conversation	73
Appendix B: Our Conversational Norms	75
Works Consulted & Recommended Reading	77
About the Author	81

The Cultivating Communities Series

Our human bodies bear witness to the truth of our lives: to the many sorts of care we have given them or to joys and traumas that they have survived. Similarly, social bodies also bear witness. They take the shape of their members' desires, convictions, and stories. And our churches are no exception. Ideally, our congregations will take a shape that bears witness to the life, death, resurrection, and teachings of Jesus. But all too often that witness is distorted by other loves and other desires in the midst of church communities that don't look a whole lot like Jesus of Nazareth. Nationalism and greed are two such loves that dilute and distort the Christian witness of churches.

In an age dominated by deep social divides – between the political right and left; between rich and poor; between various racial and ethnic identities, between generations; and between educational backgrounds, to name just a few

– how is it even possible that a church might have any shape at all beyond the nearly amorphous form taken by the loose network of her individual members?

Beyond these deep divides and the existential threat they pose to our congregations, I am hopeful churches can still mature into the full stature of a body that bears a striking resemblance to Jesus. This maturing is a slow process that will not only take time but also hard work and intentionality. What shape will our individual bodies take if we neglect to care for their physical and mental well-being? Similarly, our churches must be attentive to tending and cultivating our life together, seeking day-by-day, month-by-month, and year-by-year to more fully embody Jesus together in our particular place. This work of patient cultivation lies at the heart of **congregational formation.**

In many ways the contours of congregational formation parallel those of personal spiritual formation. Both congregational and personal formation are driven by the desire to more fully know and embody Jesus, and both take the shape of intentional practices that serve to form us into Christlikeness. However, congregational formation can be particularly messy because it requires the alignment of the desires of multiple people, not just one person. Efforts to align desires by emotional manipulation, or by more authoritarian tactics, will undoubtedly fail with time because their means are decidedly *not* those of the patient love and compassion of Jesus. In these cases, formation does happen, but the shape that is emerging looks little like Jesus.

Indeed, congregational formation occurs as we learn to be attentive to God's presence in us and among us in the Holy Spirit. We learn through a multitude of practices, especially conversation, to share our convictions, our hopes, and our stories together. And we learn to receive one another with gratitude as a vital means of God's provision for shaping and sustaining our life together. Just as our personal bodies constantly adapt, discern, mature, and move through the world as an intricate network of conversations, so also conversation becomes the way that our churches discern together who our members are, how we will care for our collective body, and how we strive to embody Christ together in ways that our neighbors see and become curious about the way of Jesus.

This new Cultivating Communities Series of books serves to offer churches tools for the long journey of congregational formation. These books are intended as field guides to help orient your congregation through essential conversations on this journey. This series is the fruit of a collaborative effort between Cultivating Communities (an initiative designed to assist churches in the work of congregational formation, based at Englewood Christian Church in Indianapolis), Missio Alliance, and the Ekklesia Project. Cultivating Communities is funded by a grant from the Lilly Endowment's Thriving Congregations Initiative, and a portion of this generous funding has been used to launch this new series of books.

The first book in this series, *The Shape of Our Lives*, was published in October 2024 and is a revised and updated edition of a resource originally produced in 2008 by the Ekklesia Project, which introduces the key elements and dynamics of congregational formation. Written by a team of pastors and theological/biblical scholars, including Phil Kenneson, Deborah Dean Murphy, Jenny Williams, Stephen Fowl, and James Lewis, *The Shape of Our Lives* serves not only as a primer on congregational formation, but also a theological backdrop for the subsequent books in this series.

The Virtue of Dialogue is the second book in the series. It builds upon our conviction that conversation is the central practice of congregational formation and recounts the earliest years of Englewood Christian Church's journey of learning to grow together in conversation. We hope this story will provide imagination for many churches about how they might learn to talk and grow together within their own particular contexts.

Subsequent volumes in the series will address specific key facets of congregational formation, including how to read scripture together, how to think and talk about money in our congregations, and more. Each volume will incorporate discussion questions intended to spark conversation. Although each book can be read and reflected on by individual church leaders, this series is primarily intended to be read, prayed over, and discussed by groups within a congregation, including perhaps in some settings, the congregation as a whole. We hope the very form of these books is consistent with and serves to cultivate vital congregational conversations.

C. Christopher Smith
Series Editor

Cultivating Communities Series Partners

Cultivating Communities is a growing network of people committed to place-based congregational formation. Our team is committed to walking with congregations who desire to cultivate a deeper life together in Christ, which overflows into tangible love for the communities in which they are embedded. Cultivating Communities is funded by a grant from the Lilly Endowment's Thriving Congregations Initiative.

Learn more at **CultivatingCommunities.com.**

The Ekklesia Project is a community of Christians from across the ecclesial spectrum who have found life-giving friendship through a shared hope in the vision of God's good shalom. In the early 2000s, the Ekklesia Project launched the Congregational Formation Initiative (CFI) to nurture and support congregations committed to making lifelong formation and discipleship central to their life together.

Connect online at **EkklesiaProject.org.**

Missio Alliance is a Managing Partner in the Cultivating Communities initiative. Founded in 2011, Missio Alliance offers in-depth theological and practical direction for many pastors and church leaders attempting to navigate the challenges of ministry in a culturally dynamic, post-Christianizing era.

Learn more at **MissioAlliance.org.**

The Kingdom of God is not in the wisdom of the world, nor in eloquence, but in the faith of the cross and in the virtue of dialogue.
— St. Cyprian

Good communities are spaces where people love one another enough that they're not afraid of disagreements. ... People that are together to be together, that's just another name for hell, as Sartre well understood. You never are together [simply] to be together, you're together because you have something you want to do, work that [needs to be done].
— Stanley Hauerwas, *Conflict vs. Comfort*

Preface

In 2012, this little book became the first piece I published on Englewood Christian Church's weekly practice of conversation. It set the stage for my books *Slow Church* (2014, co-written with John Pattison), *Reading for the Common Good* (2016), and especially *How the Body of Christ Talks* (2019), an in-depth exploration of the practice of conversation for churches.

However, even after a dozen years, when someone wants to know about our practice of conversation at Englewood—how we got started and what it means for us—I still point them to this book. It remains a clear and concise introduction to our congregational experience with talking to one another. It also challenges readers to consider what a practice of conversation might look like within the context of their own particular churches.

I am often asked about where our Sunday conversation has gone over the years since this book was written and where it stands today. Like the history of the Ancient Israelites told over the pages of the Hebrew scriptures (which Christians know as the Old Testament), our journey with conversation has been anything but linear. Three steps forward, two steps back, a season of spinning in circles and not going anywhere at all, and so on. To the frustration of some members, every few years we inevitably find ourselves in a conversation about why we talk together and how we might do it better. Personally, I think these sort of evaluative conversations are helpful, but we tend to get mired in them for way too long.

In a life together often full-to-overflowing with conversations, it can sometimes be easy to lose sight of the role our practice of regular weekly conversation plays. It is not just a niche where like-minded folks gather to discuss their work on this project or that one, or to study a portion of scripture or an important theological work (although we have plenty of these kinds of conversations at Englewood). Rather, it is a space all members—and visitors too—are invited into, one in which we struggle together to make sense of who we are as a body knit together by God. Just like our human bodies, our church body is an interconnected network of diverse members (diverse ages, diverse ethnic and religious backgrounds, diverse vocations, diverse political perspectives, and on and on.) And just like our physical bodies, our church body is healthiest when its members are paying careful attention to one another and learning to work together in spite of our differences.

Our weekly Sunday conversation is also a vital place in which we orient new members to the practice of talking together. If they are able to stick with us in the Sunday conversation for weeks or months, they will get a decent understanding of who we are and how we strive to embody the way of Jesus together in this particular urban neighborhood. I hope they see that this way of conversation, although it encourages everyone to contribute, is primarily about learning to listen. Simultaneously, we sharpen our capacity for paying attention to one another and to the time and the place in which we find ourselves gathered together by God. We certainly aren't a perfect embodiment of these aspirations, but I hope that in our conversations, visitors and new members are able to catch at least occasional glimpses of the loving, attentive, and compassionate life of Jesus unfolding in our midst.

It might be easy for outsiders to look at who Englewood Christian Church is today–and to find us so peculiar and so unlike most churches—that they dismiss our story as not having any relevance for their own church. But once upon a time, not all that long ago, we were a fairly standard evangelical church. This little book tells the story of how we began to become the peculiar sort of congregation we are today. We had no idea where the journey of conversation would take us, but we committed to the slow and often messy work of talking together.

Currently, we find ourselves in another season of reflecting on why we talk together and how we might do so in ways that invite the participation of more of our members. We don't plan these sorts of reflective conversations, but it seems like we find ourselves in them every five years or so. Sometimes the forms change a bit—we've gathered, for instance, at different times and in different spaces over the years—but we continue to talk together and to seek to know the ways in which God is guiding us. After over 25 years of our Sunday conversation, we still commit ourselves to doing this communal work.

For the last decade, I have coached distance runners of various ages, and I find a lot of parallels between running and the practice of conversation. Our Sunday conversations at Englewood aren't the big, flashy achievement, like the personal record we set for ourselves or the marathon that earns us a medal for completing. Rather, they are more akin to the hundreds of daily, routine workouts without which the big achievements wouldn't happen. Yes, we have accomplished many things over the last quarter century, but it is routine things like conversation and caring daily for one another and our neighbors that have enabled us to do so. These everyday practices form us and strengthen us in preparation for when opportunities arise to do more extraordinary things together.

I hope you find this portion of our story—how we began and waded into the practice of conversation—challenging. Particularly, I hope it might encourage you to reflect on what a regular practice of conversation might look like in your own church.

Chris

6 January 2025
Feast of the Epiphany

Introduction

Americans have used wealth and technology to invent and secure places of minimal conflict. They spend more time with people like themselves. Politicians are sharply partisan, mirroring the homogeneity of the electorate.
— Bill Bishop

For over 20 years, my family and I have lived in the Englewood neighborhood on the Near Eastside of Indianapolis. Englewood has followed a similar trajectory to many urban neighborhoods across the United States that were abandoned during the so-called white flight of the second half of the twentieth century. The two major industrial complexes that sandwiched our neighborhood on its north and south ends saw the life drained out of them over the 1980s and were finally shuttered in the early 1990s. The exodus of families and small businesses from the neighborhood paralleled the industrial decline here. A decade ago, Englewood sat at the heart of the ZIP code with the highest rate of vacant housing in the state of Indiana. But over the last twelve years, the neighborhood has begun to see some changes.

On Rural Street, the century-old Indianapolis Public School #3 building, which had not functioned as a school since 1979, was converted into thirty-two units of gorgeous, mixed-income housing. This apartment complex, which opened in 2012, was the first development in the state of Indiana to integrate market rate and affordable housing with supportive housing for people coming directly out of homelessness or severe mental illness. And not only were the classrooms of the former school transformed into fashionable apartments with high ceilings, wood floors, and lots of natural light, the building also features a three-level gymnasium and recreational facility that serves the residents and neighborhood at large.

One block east of the former school building is Oxford Street, which was almost completely vacant at the turn of the millennium. Over the last two-and-a-half decades, its empty houses have been occupied one-by-one until a majority of the homes are now filled. Neighbors in another part of the neighborhood, a few blocks away, started a block club that grew and thrived into one of the most active on our side of the city. The neighbors on this block work together on issues pertinent to the area and celebrate together with two large block parties each year.

On the south edge of the Englewood neighborhood, one of the most toxic abandoned industrial sites on the east side of Indianapolis was remediated, and its land was renewed and prepared for safe use again at a cost of over one million dollars. On this remediated land, two buildings of affordable senior housing were built within the last decade. And adjacent to the senior housing, a former industrial site was renovated five years ago into an award-winning, modern facility that houses two charter schools.

Washington Street, a major East-West thoroughfare through Indianapolis, cuts right through Englewood, and over the last decade signs of new life are beginning to emerge along it. The branch of the Indianapolis Public Library here, a historic Carnegie library built in the early twentieth century, was carefully renovated and expanded. The renovation project included adding an elevator, so that the library would be accessible, and enlarging the computer lab to better serve neighbors. The two buildings next to the library once housed a seedy used appliance dealer before being vacated around 2010. One of those buildings is now one of the most celebrated Mexican bistros in Indianapolis, which was just featured on the Food Network. The other building was also renovated, and a local artist painted an exterior mural with historical scenes from the amusement park that graced the Englewood neighborhood a century ago. It now houses a thriving educational non-profit that works with students in local schools, including the new high school across the street.

What's making all these changes possible after decades of economic downturn? One major contributor is our church community, Englewood Christian Church, whose building is situated just north of the former IPS School #3.

How is it that this modest church of less than 200 members, a failed mega-church that spiraled downward with the neighborhood, has come to help orchestrate these threads of change? I will tell that story over the course of the following chapters, but the short answer is that we learned to talk to each other. Amidst a nation that is sorting itself into homogeneous ghettos and finding civil dialogue impossible, a community is talking across deep divides and orchestrating a movement of transformation in its own neighborhood.

In his extraordinary 2008 book, *The Big Sort: Why The Clustering of Like-Minded America is Tearing Us Apart*, journalist Bill Bishop, in conjunction with sociologist Robert Cushing, describes American society over the last thirty-five years as sorting itself into increasingly homogeneous social circles. Bishop begins his book:

> [In] every corner of society, people were creating new, more homogeneous relations. Churches were filled with people who looked alike and, more important, thought alike. So were clubs, civic organizations, and volunteer groups. Social psychologists had studied like-minded groups and could predict how people living and worshipping in homogeneous groups would react: as people heard their beliefs reflected and amplified, they would become more extreme in their thinking.

And as the convictions of citizens bent toward the extremes in recent decades, they gradually lost the capacity for civil conversation with those of differing perspectives. Over the latter half of the era Bishop examined, the geographical sorting was amplified by the rise of internet technologies into which many people poured increasing amounts of time and energy, typically seeking out conversations with people around the globe who shared similar convictions or practices. This emerging internet culture only served to energize the social divisions already underway in the United States.

In the midst of this atmosphere of fragmentation, Englewood Christian Church, one congregation among many in our neighborhood, carved out some time on our Sunday nights and began to talk together. As we talked, we began to build trust among ourselves. Eventually, these conversations overflowed Sunday nights and began popping up throughout the week, and our church community also began finding ways to converse with our neighbors. And out of these conversations, things began to get done—not just impulsive acts ignited by a "just do something" reaction, but meaningful acts flowing out of the convictions that—after the dust we kicked up during the struggles of our conversations settled—we found we shared in common.

What follows is the story of these conversations, an account that includes how we were and continue to be changed by the process of talking together, and how these conversations have led to the tiniest ripples of transformative change in our neighborhood. We are broken people in the midst of a profoundly broken neighborhood, and conversation has not been a quick fix for any of our problems; yet, God continues to meet us in the middle of our conversations and slowly and patiently transforms us. Most, if not all, church congregations long to experience the reconciling presence of God in their midst, and also out of that center of divine reconciliation to begin to spread Christ's love to their neighbors. I share this story here out of our deep conviction that conversation is an essential practice for the people of God. As we learn to set aside our personal agendas and talk together in Christ-like ways, God is at work behind the scenes shaping us into the reconciled body of Christ.

Congregational conversations might take forms as different as the places our churches inhabit, but God's people are all called to share life together, gradually coming to know others and to allow ourselves to be known. At the heart of this life of communion is conversation. I hope our story will be a means of God's grace for your church, challenging you and ultimately blessing you. May God give us all the courage to buck the incivility and fragmentation of our times.

Chapter One

The Rise and Fall of an Urban Mega-Church: Setting the Stage for Conversation

When this congregation was founded, it had a suburban image, and through the years, it has maintained a suburban image. But now we realize that we are not suburban; we are urban.

— Richard Laue, Englewood Pastor
"From Rural Street to Urban Avenue" Sermon
20 October 1968

Although I have been part of the Englewood Christian Church community for about twenty years, I have been immersed here in the stories of a much longer history. The individualism of Western culture often obscures this reality, but storytelling is one of the primary ways communities historically have shaped the identity of their members.

In this way, my immersion into the stories of Englewood has formed in me an identity that helps me fit within this community of people in this particular place. Therefore, I frequently use personal pronouns—"we," "us," "our"—when I talk about the history of Englewood. These are the stories of the people to which I belong, and in that sense, they are my stories as well.

In November 1895, when Grover Cleveland was President and the first U.S. patents for automobiles had just been issued, a church was founded. Members had established a few years of modestly successful Bible studies, and they began to gather more formally in a commercial space located across Rural Street from where our building stands today. Rural Street, like many suburban streets, was probably named as an idyllic and sentimental connection to a quickly fading past. The Englewood neighborhood was then in the early stages of its development as a suburb of Indianapolis and largely was populated by people moving outward from the city center, which at the time had a growing immigrant population.

Within five years of its start, the church had broken ground for a permanent facility. The church grew rapidly over its first quarter-century, and in these early years was a neighborhood church with a stable family-oriented congregation, reflecting the white, middle-class demographics of the neighborhood. By the late 1920s, it was one of the most prominent churches nationwide in our fellowship of churches.[1] In 1927, it hosted the fellowship's very first North American Christian Convention, an annual gathering that continued for almost a century, until just a few years ago. During the first half of our church's life, we were led by a string of energetic and popular pastors and, perhaps more importantly, a strong board comprised mostly of businessmen and other neighborhood leaders.

In the late 1920s, two industrial complexes emerged that would sandwich the Englewood neighborhood, both focused on the production of electronic devices: to the north was Westinghouse, which would soon become RCA, and to the south was the P.R. Mallory Company. RCA and Mallory provided a solid economic foundation for the neighborhood that would last for almost fifty years. (It was at Mallory that the Duracell battery was developed and branded in the 1960s).

Following World War II, the neighborhood began a gradual season of change as the G.I. Bill offered returning soldiers incentives to buy new homes, but *not* to fix up existing homes. So began the first trickle of families moving out of the neighborhood to new suburban communities farther out from the city center.

Throughout the mid-twentieth century, our church continued to grow, even as the neighborhood began to change around it. With church growth, however, came a shift in the makeup of the congregation; it was no longer primarily a neighborhood church. People drove in from all over the city. Many members who had moved out of the neighborhood came back for Sunday services, and the church had a bus ministry to bring in children and their families from a wide swath of the city. The young and energetic pastor of that time hosted a popular radio show that also attracted people.

Our church fit well in the sort of 1960s evangelicalism in which the church growth movement burgeoned, and grow it did, by some accounts reaching as much as 3,000 members in the early 1970s—although church records show average Sunday attendance maxing out around 1,100, with as many as 1,500 on special occasions. In contrast, during the late 1960s, as Englewood was climbing to its largest size, most Protestant churches consisted of fewer than 75 members.

Beginning in this same era, the late 1960s, the economic and racial demographics of Englewood and surrounding neighborhoods began to change more rapidly than in the previous two decades, precipitating the sort of "white flight" to the suburbs that has been documented in cities throughout the U.S. Many churches also followed their members outward from the city centers. In the mid-1970s, the pastor who had successfully guided our church through its most explosive period of growth left. His leaving, coinciding with the broader exodus from the neighborhood, set the size of the congregation into a freefall. Attendance plummeted rapidly from the late-1970s into the 1980s, until it finally bottomed out at fewer than 200 people.

The period from the mid-1970s to the early 1990s was also marked by rapid changes in the pastoral leadership of the church. Not only was the shift made from a single pastor to a staff of several pastors, but there was also much turnover in these leadership positions. Each new pastor brought with him a new agenda and theology, with the hopes of fixing the struggling church. The challenges that our church faced in this era, however, were not the sort that could be fixed with any type of trendy program or technique, and the pastors would eventually give up and leave the church. Often, when one of these pastors left, he would take some of the congregation with him, and even those left behind became increasingly fragmented by the various theologies that lingered in the church community. Some clung to the traditional Christian Church theology of earlier decades; many were interested in the latest evangelical trends and programs; others were deeply invested in charismatic renewal.

As the congregation fragmented and approached its smallest size in decades, our leaders needed to make a decision about whether the church would stay put in its now decidedly urban location or would follow many sister churches in their migration to the suburbs further east. At this crucial point in our history, church leadership decided we would stay rooted in our historic location. This commitment launched us on a journey of seeking what it means to love our neighbors in this place. If God indeed wanted us to remain here, we trusted God would continue to guide us and provide the resources we would need to do the work to which we had been called.

One of our first responses was to launch a number of "pantry" ministries typical of many urban churches and para-church groups: a food pantry, a clothing pantry, and even a furniture pantry. These ministries ran for about a decade, from the early 1980s to the early 1990s. As the years progressed, however, we found that we were helping to transfer a lot of goods—much of which came from our sister churches in suburbia—but were not connecting with the people to whom the goods were given. This work was not only failing to nurture friendships with our neighbors, it was also creating destructive dynamics of need and dependency, and for these reasons, we eventually shut it down.

It was in this context that we came—or perhaps more accurately, stumbled—into the practice of conversation.

Although Englewood was once a prestigious church, the pride of our fellowship of churches, and once a mega-church, we were now neither large nor influential. Rather, we were a church that had plunged toward destruction as many abandoned our neighborhood, and the church members who remained were deeply fragmented by the leadership turnover and strategy shifts mentioned above. In this era, very few church members lived in our neighborhood, and in many ways we had become more like a center for urban ministry than a church congregation.

It seemed we were on the verge of dying as a church, but like the tree that is stripped bare for the winter before it can be resurrected and flourish in the spring, we were only weathering a wintry season. God was preparing us for a sort of resurrection.

Discussion Questions

1. Think about the state of dialogue in our society as a whole. How would you describe it? What obstacles do you see to good, productive conversations? On the other hand, what are some examples of God-honoring dialogue you *have* seen, and what made it valuable and worthwhile?

2. What do you know about the history of your church? How long have you been a part of the congregation? What parts of the church's history do you feel a part of, and which do you feel more distance from?

3. This chapter refers to a season in Englewood Church Church's history as a type of winter, preparing for resurrection. Reflect on the winter seasons in the life of your church or your own individual life. What new things were birthed after those seasons?

---

1. Englewood Christian Church is part of the Christian Churches [Churches of Christ] or, as they are sometimes called, the Independent Christian Churches, which along with the Disciples of Christ and the Non-Instrumental Churches of Christ, comprise the three streams of the Stone-Campbell tradition.

Chapter Two

Becoming Rooted Together: Our Sunday Night Conversation

Good communities are spaces where people love one another enough that they're not afraid of disagreements.

— Stanley Hauerwas

In the mid-1990s, Englewood had a Sunday night service that was little more than a "lite" version of the Sunday morning service. Like many evangelical churches of that time, we could attract little interest in that service. It was dying, but we were not ready to abandon altogether the habit of meeting on Sunday nights, so we decided to try something different.

One Sunday night in 1997, we set up a big circle of chairs and started to talk together. Taking cues from other conversations already under way in other parts of our life together, we began with the question: "What is the Word of God?" It was commonplace at that time—and still is today—for many evangelicals to speak of the Bible as the word of God. But what did the biblical writers mean when they referred to "the word of God" in passages like John 1:1 or Acts 4:31? Is there a consistent meaning for this phrase throughout the biblical texts, and if so, what is it? And with such questions, we plunged into a deep and tumultuous sea of conversation.

What would have been a tense conversation anyway was amplified by the deep fragmentation of our recent history. Like so many Western churches, we had nurtured a culture of individualized faith. Thus, when we gathered the individuals of our church community for conversation, they brought with them not only a divergent array of theological, social, and political convictions, but also deep emotional attachment to these convictions. We had some people in our congregation who were deeply committed to the convictions and practices of the Stone-Campbell tradition out of which our church was formed. Others were thoroughgoing Evangelicals, who advocated for the latest ideas and programs promoted by evangelical media outlets like Focus on the Family and *Christianity Today*. Another segment of our church was deeply committed serving underprivileged neighbors around us through food, clothing, and furniture pantry programs. Another segment of the church had come of age during the Jesus people era of the 1970s, and had strong convictions about radical discipleship and sharing life together in the church. It's not too difficult to imagine that when all these groups within the congregation came together, they brought with them many conflicting ideas about what it meant to follow Jesus and to be the church.

Additionally, our congregation was embedded within a broader culture that was rapidly losing the capacity for conversation. Landmark books like Robert Putnam's *Bowling Alone* (2001) and Bill Bishop's *The Big Sort* (2009) drew upon deep reservoirs of sociological realities to highlight why Americans struggled to talk together. *Bowling Alone* painted a picture of American society that expanded upon its title image: In the late twentieth century more Americans were bowling than ever before, but at the same time bowling leagues were gradually dying off from lack of participation. Social capital, a concept that Putnam popularized, was waning, as local social groups like PTAs, bowling leagues, and even churches were declining. With the decline of participation in social groups, Americans began to lose the capacity to work through the sorts of disagreements that such groups inevitably face.

Additionally, Fred Rogers, the star of the PBS television series *Mister Rogers's Neighborhood*, and other advocates for the well-being of children and families, noted that the family dinner table diminished as a cultural institution over the second half of the twentieth century. And with the decline of the family dinner table, Americans were losing the conversational skills that the dinner table often served to form—e.g., how to disagree gracefully, or how to distribute the limited resources of the table fairly, like the last piece of fried chicken or the final slice of pie.

Bill Bishop's book *The Big Sort* tracked political identities in American communities over the final quarter of the twentieth century, and found that Americans were increasingly living in places where their neighbors largely shared their convictions. This geographical sorting meant Americans increasingly had fewer opportunities to interact with others who did not share their convictions, and thus fewer opportunities to exercise their conversational skills in situations of substantial disagreement.

Even in the late 1990s, before the boom of the internet, our congregation at Englewood reflected the rapidly diminishing capacity for conversation that was prevalent across most of American society. A common phrase that popped up in the early years of the conversation whenever a bold idea was proposed—say, that the "word of God" might be more than just the Bible or that God's work of salvation might be bigger than saving individual souls—was, "You can't say that!"

We were a people who had been formed by the powers at work in our church and in the culture at large[1], and it quickly became apparent we did not know how to talk to each other. Our conversation in those earliest years was extraordinarily volatile. People frequently got angry and yelled at others; some would get up and walk out. The conflict was intense, and not everyone was prepared to handle it. Some members quit coming on Sunday nights.

One of the most volatile streams of our conversation was our discussion of the nature of salvation. This is not surprising, because salvation is a concept that lies close to the heart of evangelical Christianity. Among the people in the conversation were some who clung tightly to traditional evangelical understandings of personal salvation, who refused to fathom that God's work of reconciling a rebellious creation might be broader than securing eternal life for us as individuals. To question the meaning of salvation as we did elicited great anxiety, and several people left the church as a result of this part of our conversation.

My wife and I first came to Englewood eight years into the Sunday night conversations. The tone was still often harsh and sarcastic. My wife's comment to me after her first Sunday night conversation was: "These people don't even like each other."

Despite the conflict that raged, a sense of commitment emerged over time among those who remained—a commitment to one another and to God's work in this place, which ran deeper than the depths of our disagreements. The ongoing effect of the Sunday night conversation was that we were beginning to love and trust each other in meaningful ways; love was gradually becoming something more than a hollow, religious word to us. We also were slowly learning to talk together. A vernacular was taking shape, a local language rooted in the shared convictions about the nature of God's creation and what God was doing in our midst.

The Sunday night conversation was facilitated by a member who was not a pastor of the church. He had grown up in the church at Englewood but was never at home in the prevailing evangelicalism of earlier decades, having at one point even been kicked out of Bible college. To his credit, he stuck with the church over several decades of his adult life, despite his critical opinions about the church's evangelicalism and how that theology was worked out in the shared practices of the church.

His role as facilitator was to get the conversation rolling and prod it when it slowed down. A gifted critic and provocateur, he did well at keeping the conversation moving along, but like everyone else in the room, he came into the conversation with an agenda. Because he was the facilitator his agenda, which was critical of the evangelical status quo, sometimes served more to inflame than to help the church community mature into the fullness of Christ. In the prevailing culture of "You can't say that!" no one wanted to say what he or she really thought. In order to get people talking, our facilitator inserted his own thoughts in bold terms that were often critical and sarcastic. He found himself in a difficult place, because this sort of provocation stirred up much hostility, but it also got us moving into meaningful conversation about what we believed.

The earliest years of the conversations were spent trying to understand how a number of familiar terms were used in the Bible and what they meant for the shape of our life together in this place. From the initial focus on "the word of God," the conversation eventually turned to an exploration of what the Gospel is (a task not unlike that undertaken in Scot McKnight's recent book, *The King Jesus Gospel*), and from there to questions about the nature of salvation (is it more than the individualistic notion of "accepting Jesus into my heart," and if so, what is it?). Later, we spent a long time discussing truth: Is there such a thing as absolute or objective truth, and what did Jesus mean when he said, "I am the way, the truth and the life," (John 14:6)? Still later, we discussed the kingdom of God and its implications for our identity and allegiances as followers of Christ.

A key facet of many of our conversations was the struggle to understand the church's role in God's redemptive work, and toward this end we spent a lot of time discussing Ephesians, including six months on Ephesians 4:7-16. This is a crucial passage for understanding the life together to which we have been called as churches, and how the gifts God has given each of us (verse 7) work together to help our local church body mature "into the fullness of Christ" (verse 13). As the conversation moved forward, many common assumptions about modern American culture were scrutinized in the light of the Gospel of Jesus—individualism, nationalism, objectivity, consumerism—and in the process, we came to see how these assumptions were inhibiting our growth and maturity as a church community.

Conversation has not been a magical solution to bring us to one-mindedness or solve all our conflicts. Today, we still do not agree on all the questions we have asked over the years, but we do agree on more and have a much deeper sense of trust that God is guiding us and will continue to work in our midst.

In recent years, our conversation has tended to be not only more civil, but also more structured. One of the first of these more structured threads focused on the question of membership. As a century-old congregation, and as one that had historically been significantly larger, we often met people at neighborhood meetings or in other contexts who claimed to be members of Englewood, but whom no one in the church could remember. Additionally, the theological shifts underway were gradually transforming our convictions about salvation and discipleship, and thus also were impacting our understanding of membership. We therefore set out on a quest to define what it meant to be a member of our church, beginning with exploration of the membership commitments made by sister churches and intentional Christian communities across a wide swath of church traditions. We surveyed the membership covenants, commitments, and practices of traditional churches here in Indianapolis, as well as in other places, and those of intentional Christian communities—such as Reba Place Fellowship in Evanston, Illinois—who make deep commitments to one another when they become members.

Our conversations with other churches led to further dialogue among ourselves about the sorts of commitments we would make together in Christ. These conversations eventually led to the writing of a membership covenant, and then a seemingly endless conversation to refine and wordsmith it, producing a covenant on which we all could agree. This conversation on membership, including the writing of our covenant, took over a year and a half, and even today we still are learning and exploring how the covenant will function in our life together—how we will commit ourselves to it and submit ourselves to be formed by it.

In perhaps the most structured era of our Sunday night conversation, we worked our way through the curriculum of the Ekklesia Project's Congregational Formation Initiative, which was intended to help congregations recognize and mature into their calling as communities of God's people. This study reinforced many of our previous conversations about the nature of the church and continued to challenge and refine the theological language we use in our conversations.

Most recently, we have spent over two years reflecting on a series of questions originally posed at our annual retreat in 2009. These questions were aimed at helping us discern a clearer sense of our calling as a church in our particular place and with the particular people that God has provided us; they moved from the general—"What is God doing in and with the world?"—to more specific questions like "How has God chosen to accomplish God's mission in the world?" to very particular questions about our common life as Englewood Christian Church that explored what we have been called to be and do together. (A list of these questions has been included as an appendix at the back of this book.)

By sitting down together every Sunday night in that circle, we began the long, slow process of learning how to converse; we built trust, hammered out the foundations of a shared language, and deepened our commitments to one another. Our Sunday night conversation was like the root system of a rhizome plant like ginger or bamboo, which has an immense underground network of roots and stems, and only occasionally has a stem that emerges from the earth's surface. Our conversation deepened and intertwined over the years, providing stability to our life together, but still remained largely underground, confined within the walls of the church building and among church members. However, as the Sunday night conversation progressed, a number of offshoot conversations began to appear and these discussions were—like the shoots of the rhizome—more visible and public in nature. In these new conversations, we were called deeper into the transforming work that God is doing in our urban neighborhood.

Discussion Questions

1. What role do dialogue and conversation play in your congregation? What important conversations have been had in the past, and what were their outcomes?

2. Are there important conversations that need to be had within your church community? How can space be made for these conversation to happen?

3. Where in scripture do you see evidence of how God values conversation? What instruction or insight does this provide regarding how you approach conversation in Christian community?

4. Reflect back on your life and spiritual journey so far. Are any conversations particularly memorable? How have those conversations contributed to your personal and spiritual formation, for good or for ill?

---

1. For a deeper exploration of the powers that shape congregational life, see the first book in this Cultivating Communities Series, *The Shape of Our Lives: A Field Guide for Congregational Formation.*

Chapter Three

Becoming a Conversational People: Talking Together Throughout the Week

You never are together [simply] to be together, you're together because you have something you want to do, work that [needs to be done].

— Stanley Hauerwas

When my wife and I joined Englewood Christian Church in the summer of 2003, we found that becoming part of the church community meant immersing ourselves in a number of ongoing conversations. And although the Sunday night conversation was deeply theological, the conversations we encountered in the church were as varied as the activities in which its members were involved, from childcare, to finance, to housing, to food, to many other facets of life. As the church had learned to talk together on Sunday nights, it was catapulted into many other conversations that spanned the week. Few topics were off-limits, including the beliefs and operations of the church.

In the past, many of the church's decisions were made in closed-door board meetings. Over time, the church's board meeting morphed into a ministry council meeting, which all members of the church are encouraged to attend. Many of the traditional groups within the church—Sunday School classes, small groups, etc.—have become opportunities to expand our discussions and take them in new directions. Some groups would read books together, whether books of the Bible or other titles such as Richard Hays's *Moral Vision of the New Testament*, Gerhard Lohfink's *Jesus and Community*, or Phil Kenneson's *Life on the Vine*; others would discuss topics such as missions and global issues.

Some of these conversations pre-dated the Sunday night gatherings, but talking together weekly helped change the dynamic of these discussions, allowing us to go deeper and work through difficult issues together in other contexts as we had been learning to do on Sunday nights.

Although some of the conversations were of a similar kind to those we had encountered in other churches—though perhaps more intense here—others didn't fit any of our previous church experiences. The most notable example was the opportunities created for common work throughout the week. The church created jobs for some members to work together in its early childhood education center and in its community development corporation, but common work extended beyond the limited scope of these jobs. Members also worked together in fixing up homes in the neighborhood, in tending the community garden, and other opportunities to care for one another and for the neighborhood. Working together gave our church an opportunity to know and converse with one another in a broader range of contexts, and it also gave us the opportunity to reflect theologically together and make discernments about how we as a church (a community that embodies Christ in our particular neighborhood) should do the work to which we are called. The work we have chosen to do is real work we believe God has called us into as God transforms our neighborhood and causes it to flourish. Our businesses therefore allow us to initiate and sustain conversations with neighbors and others throughout the city about the efforts in which we all are collaborators.

Our first and most successful venture in working together, a daycare and preschool, began not long after the start of the Sunday night conversation. In the late 1990s, with the rise of welfare-to-work legislation came a steep need in our urban neighborhood for good and affordable childcare. Building upon the foundation of an already-existing preschool ministry, the daycare grew steadily over the years, taking on more children and creating more job opportunities for church members and neighbors. In recent years, the daycare is recognized as one of the leading church-based daycare ministries in Central Indiana. Today, it employs over 40 people and provides care and education for over 170 children from birth through pre-kindergarten.

Another of our most successful initiatives has focused on providing affordable housing in our neighborhood. The mass exodus from our neighborhood in the last decades of the twentieth century provided a prime opportunity for us to acquire homes cheaply, fix them up, and sell or rent them to people in our congregation who were not in good housing situations. We had several people in the church community who were skilled and available to coordinate this work, including the facilitator of our Sunday night conversation—who had recently graduated from a local college with a degree in structural design—as well as a real estate agent, a real estate appraiser, and others. As we continued to work on housing, we were drawn into substantial conversations with other groups doing community development work, with neighborhood groups, with other churches in the neighborhood whose members needed housing, and with a variety of city and state agencies.

Three years ago, we were given a former public school building located next door to our church, which prompted a long series of conversations about how that facility should best be used, and how the needed work should be funded. Many of us thought the building should again be home to a school, but conversations with schools fizzled. It eventually became clear we should redevelop the building as housing units, but how would we fund it, as we struggle to keep the church running, let alone such a mammoth housing complex? We eventually decided, given the lack of interest shown by schools and given the grant funding available in the wake of the burst housing bubble, the best use would be to renovate the building as thirty-two units of mixed-income rental housing, the first of its kind in Indiana. The building would include ten units for people coming directly out of homelessness or severe mental illness, fifteen units of income-capped affordable housing, and seven units of unrestricted market rate housing. This $7 million project—our largest to date by far—would not have been possible had we not already been in working conversations about affordable housing with the neighborhood and city groups that became our partners on this project.

A number of other businesses originated in the gifts and skills of church members. One member was an accountant for a large bank but wanted out of that job and to work more closely with the church, so we found bookkeeping accounts she could maintain for other local churches and nonprofits. This bookkeeping work snowballed over time and has since provided work for a handful of others. We launched a landscaping business that provides summer work for many young men in our church, and a handful of book-related businesses including a small bookstore, publishing operation, and an online book review, *The Englewood Review of Books*.

All of these businesses created some opportunities for us to work and talk together throughout the week and have launched us into a multitude of trade-related conversations with folks in our neighborhood and beyond. As a community that is becoming more thoroughly conversational, we have tried to create as many avenues as possible for members to be involved in the work we are doing, especially people who are not church employees. All our businesses seek not only to synergize the various sorts of work we are doing as a church, but they also have boards and ministry teams through which others in the congregation, who might not necessarily be employees, can speak into and be engaged in this work as much as possible. One of the loveliest examples of this sort of engagement is a group of retired men in the congregation who show up at the church building every weekday and do whatever odd jobs need to be done in the church building or for any of our businesses, from painting to hauling appliances or books to taking people to doctor's appointments and so on.

Our journey toward becoming a conversational people has also drawn us deeply into discussion with our neighbors. Since early in the history of the Sunday night conversation, we have been actively involved in a number of neighborhood groups in our immediate Englewood neighborhood and across the larger Near Eastside. We have members who have deeply invested themselves in these groups, serving on boards and committees, and we have also opened our building for many of these groups to use as a regular meeting place.

In 2007, the Near Eastside was identified by Indianapolis as a redevelopment zone. In other Indy neighborhoods, this designation has been the first step on the fast track to gentrification, a frequent urban phenomenon in which residents of poorer neighborhoods are driven out by widespread redevelopment that causes property values (and housing costs) to skyrocket. It was clear to us and our neighbors that many facets of our neighborhood could use significant investment, but the last thing we wanted to do was drive out our neighbors who already had roots in the Near Eastside.

In response to this opportunity, our church hosted a six-month-long series of meetings exploring how our neighborhood could flourish in ways that would minimize or eliminate gentrification. These neighborhood-wide conversations were recorded to form a "quality of life plan" that identified seven key action areas that the neighborhood wanted to develop: Family Strengthening, Education, Public Safety, Affordable Housing, Business and Economic Development, Livability, and Leadership and Neighborhood Connections. Within each of these seven areas, a work plan was spelled out to identify immediate and long-term goals for developing the neighborhood. This Quality of Life plan continues to serve in helping the neighborhood make decisions about what development projects should be undertaken and how they should be funded. (The Quality of Life Plan can be accessed in full at https://neareastplan.org)

For the last four years, the neighborhood has been immersed in carrying out this plan and our church has been involved in that work on a number of different levels: creating affordable housing opportunities, working on food issues, and leading the way in reimagining our Englewood neighborhood. Had it not been for the ways God prepared us as a conversational people, however, we would have never been able to engage in the redevelopment of our neighborhood in the substantial ways God has opened for us over the last five years.

Another good example of our conversational engagement in our neighborhood revolves around a number of food-related issues. Our neighborhood is a food desert, and the closest two grocery stores to the church building have closed within the last five years. Our church community has a number of agriculturally-gifted folks, and we have had a community garden for over a decade, as well as beehives on the roof of our church building and a number of fruit trees that we maintain. However, after the closing of the local grocery stores, our neighbors were increasingly interested in creating a cooperative grocery store that would provide good, local food, but also be sensitive to our lower-income neighbors.

As one can imagine, these two goals were largely at odds with each other. We had a number of our Englewood members who were deeply invested in these food co-op conversations, and again because we had been prepared through the Sunday night conversation, we were able to navigate these tricky issues and see the co-op's vision come to fruition with the opening of Pogue's Run Grocer on the Near Eastside in January of 2011. Sadly, this grocery store couldn't sustain this challenging dual focus and lasted for less than a decade, but its existence inspired a wave of other food-justice organizations and programs—urban farms, farmers' markets, and more—many of which still operate today.

Among our new conversation partners are other churches, beginning with churches in our neighborhood and extending outward throughout the city, the state, and the nation. We have taken many opportunities to work with other churches in our neighborhood, holding joint services, working together on projects and engaging together in the continuing development work of our neighborhood.

These occasions for working and talking together have created space for sharing our stories and our lives together.

In 2003, we became acquainted with Mano de Amistad, a Spanish-language church meeting in the school building next door, the same building that would later be given to us. Not long afterward, we invited them to use our church building for their meetings, and we continued to get to know them and seek opportunities to work together. The two congregations merged in 2009, and we continue to converse and grow together, although we still have a long way to go, considering for instance that we presently have two services separated by language and the culture and history of their participants (e.g., style of music, order of services, etc.).

Englewood has also been involved with a number of para-church ministries based in our neighborhood, including several homeless shelters and Outreach, Inc., a ministry that serves homeless teenagers. These relationships and particularly our relationship with Mission Indy—a group that works with young people in churches and gives them practical experience in theological reflection and urban ministry—have led us into relationships with a number of churches throughout Central Indiana. We have also hosted conferences on specific topics like new monasticism, consumerism, agriculture, and immigration featuring national speakers including Shane Claiborne, Jonathan Wilson-Hartgrove, and Daniel Carroll. These conferences have been times for churches to come from all over the country to discuss a relevant topic together, and hopefully have also spurred some conversations afterward in the churches in attendance. Our online book review, *The Englewood Review of Books*, aims to promote practices of reading and conversation in churches, and is another way we initiate conversations with other churches and encourage the practice of conversation in their particular places.

In recent years, we have also been active with a few nationwide networks of diverse churches. Foremost among these is the Ekklesia Project, a "network of Christians from across the Christian tradition who rejoice in a peculiar kind of friendship rooted in our common love of God and the Church." Our involvement with the Ekklesia Project—which includes sending a group of our members to the annual gathering in Chicago every year—allows us to participate in wider conversations about the nature and calling of the church, but also challenges us to think and live more deeply in our calling here as a community of God's people. We have also been involved with the Christian Community Development Association for more than a decade, participating in the local host team when their annual conference was in Indianapolis, and running their conference bookstore for several years. Since 2020, we have also partnered with Missio Alliance on a project called Cultivating Communities, which helps congregations across the country deepen life together within their congregations and deepen their roots in their local places.

As our life together has become more deeply rooted in our Sunday night conversation, we find ourselves drawn into a conversational way of life that is not simply passive discussion but rather full of life and of careful activity. This is one contributing factor in our neighborhood's process of beginning to change and flourish. We believe conversation is essential to the sort of abundant life together into which we have been called in Christ Jesus. Although their practices of conversation and the activity ignited in these discussions may look vastly different from our experiences at Englewood, churches can and should be creating spaces for conversation, and as they do, they will find God moving in their midst and transforming their neighborhoods.

Discussion Questions

1. Take some time to discuss the story of Englewood Christian Church in Indianapolis. What strikes you about this story? Are there any events or developments that are reminiscent of your own church's story? What differences do you see?

2. What opportunities do you, as an individual, have for dialogue with your literal neighbors? Do you ever hear from them about their needs, their desires, or their relationship with the neighborhood/community/city? What would it look like for conversations with your neighbors to deepen or become more meaningful?

3. Consider the idea of "common work." Is this a practice familiar to your or your congregation? What needs exist in your community or neighborhood? Do members of your congregation bring any particular expertise, curiosity, or experience that makes them well-suited to meet those needs?

4. If your faith community chose to engage in some common work, what needs could be met? What outcomes can you imagine?

Chapter Four

A Space for All to be Heard: The Hospitality of Conversation

"[Hospitality] emerges from a willingness to create time and space for people"

— Christine Pohl

Even in the 1960s and 1970s when Englewood Christian Church was a very large congregation—and long before we began our practice of Sunday conversation—one of its hallmarks as a congregation was its hospitality. In that era, the church owned three houses adjacent to its building, and one of those houses was designated as a hospitality house, where missionaries could stay during furloughs or other visitors could make a brief stay. In the same era, one of the other houses was home to several young men in the congregation, who would occasionally welcome neighbors who were homeless or struggling with addiction to stay with them temporarily. The third house was right next door to the church building and originally was built as a parsonage for the church's pastor, but it ceased to be used for this purpose in the mid-1970s and sat vacant for many years. In the early 1990s, the congregation decided to renovate it and use it as a larger hospitality house, and this house continues to function as a vital part of the church's practice of hospitality today.

In the 1980s, the congregation welcomed a family of Hmong refugees from Laos, who fled their homeland in the tumultuous years after the Laotian civil war. The church provided housing for this family, and helped them learn English, find work, and adjust to American society. Some family members became part of the congregation, while others, as time went on, became less connected to it.

These stories, and many others that could be told, emphasize that hospitality was historically a central part of our life together at Englewood. As our practice of conversation emerged in the late 1990s, it is not surprising that despite the volatility of these conversations, they also became another avenue for us to extend hospitality to neighbors, visitors, and even to one another.

Common conceptions of hospitality depict two distinct roles: host (the one who is extending hospitality) and guest (the recipient of the hospitality). While Christian traditions and practices of hospitality certainly include this dynamic, they reflect the image of Christ when they go beyond this dichotomy to create spaces of mutuality in which gifts flow in both directions. Christine Pohl, whose book *Making Room* is an essential work on the practice of Christian hospitality, notes that "practitioners consistently comment that they receive more than they give." At Englewood, although the church community as a whole functions as the host of our conversations, there are a multitude of guests from both inside and outside the congregation, and the lines defining host and guest are often blurred.

Pohl describes Christian hospitality:

> In hospitality, the stranger [or guest] is welcomed into a safe, personal, and comfortable place, a place of respect and acceptance and friendship. Even if only briefly, the stranger is included in a life-giving and life-sustaining

> network of relations. Such welcome involves attentive listening and a mutual sharing of lives and life stories. It requires an openness of heart, a willingness to make one's life visible to others, and a generosity of time and resources.

Although our practice of conversation has never fully embodied the sort of hospitality that Pohl describes, at some point our historical practices of hospitality aligned with our emerging practice of conversation, and we came to aspire to have our weekly conversations be this kind of hospitable space.

We regularly welcome visitors and neighbors into this space, as well as people within our congregation who are new or on the margins of our community, and invite everyone to participate together in exploring the current topic of conversation. At one point, our church building sat adjacent to three homeless shelters, and it was a regular occurrence for a neighbor staying at one of these shelters to wander into our building on a Sunday evening, looking for a worship service. Such guests were encouraged to participate, but a few times we had to stage awkward interventions when a guest would try to derail the conversation at length with whatever thoughts were rolling through their mind. In some of those cases, someone from the church would offer to continue the conversation about what was on the guest's mind at another time. We did typically want to hear that person out, but also recognized that their thoughts flowed in a different direction than that which we were pursuing in our congregational conversations.

Inherent in hospitality is a tension between the aims of the host and those of the guest, something Pohl names as "the fragility of hospitality." She tells the story of a church to which she once belonged that saw its primary vocation as hospitality, a congregation that strived to respond faithfully to the needs of all neighbors who crossed its path. "It was an incredibly fruitful and blessed time," she writes. "Within only a few years, however, the church itself had collapsed under the weight of ministry, the leaders worn out from the unrelenting numbers of needy strangers, the parishioners wary of any further commitments." We often recognized this sort of tension in our practice of conversation. We want to be generous in receiving guests in our conversations, in the same spirit of hospitality God extends to us in Jesus. At the same time, the conversations are a necessary practice for us inside the congregation, and we also have to be faithful to the ways we are caring for one another and growing together as a particular expression of Christ's body. Navigating this tension requires patience, gentleness, and kindness, and an agreed-upon set of conversational norms to which we can refer back when necessary.

If someone were to arrive at a Sunday evening conversation at Englewood, they would see chairs arranged in a large circle and a handwritten list of "conversational norms" on the wall. We call the room "The Parlor," and though it's an informal multi-purpose space, even the name implies a space built for and focused on conversation. A rotating team of people are responsible for transcribing and taking notes on every week, which are then provided via email for all church members. Any congregation that wishes to implement a conversation practice will need to think carefully about the unique individuals who make up their specific community. For example, are there language differences that might require translation and interpretation? Do members with hearing or speech impairments require accommodation to participate fully? Hospitality and inclusion are not limited to these practical considerations, but they are certainly necessary to consider. The choice of space, arrangement of the room, and format of our time together are all conscious decisions we have made to foster the type of conversation we desire to have.

The type of hospitality that was cultivated as we continued to practice conversation—and particularly as we extended it to one another within our church—is a sort that is rarely found in twenty-first century churches. Specifically, it was a space where all members were welcome and invited to be seen and heard, and not just once or occasionally, but week after week, year after year, as we each continued to learn and grow. In the spirit of hospitality, our Sunday conversations were not driven or orchestrated by our pastors. In many American churches, the closest approximation of this dynamic happens in small groups (which are often called life groups, home groups, community groups, etc.). These groups can provide a tiny taste of this kind of hospitality, but necessarily only for the tiny segment of the congregation within a particular group and not for the congregation as a whole.

At Englewood, it felt essential that our conversations were experienced by and contributed to by as large a portion of our church as possible. Being seen and heard is vital for cultivating our personal belonging in a particular community, and for the flourishing of a community as it grows in its understanding of its members and their gifts. Some participants in our conversations exhibited, over time, gifts in carefully reading scripture and interpreting what it might mean for us today. And it's important to note that these gifts didn't always line up with academic training: some members cultivated these gifts over years of practice in the local church context. Other members demonstrated gifts in careful listening and asking good questions. As we eventually expanded to a team approach in facilitating our conversations, we would draw upon these gifts that were uncovered in the course of our talking together. Even certain anxieties some members had—about scarcity or ambiguity, for instance—were, in an indirect way, their own sort of gifts that taught us to move slowly and be attentive to these concerns that arose among us. As an increasingly ideologically diverse community, we are slowly learning to receive the gifts of both our more conservative and more progressive members. Our conservative siblings remind us, among other things, that history and tradition matter and we should not hastily abandon them. On the other hand, our progressive siblings teach us not to simply settle for the *status quo*, that God is at work transforming not only us as a congregation, but indeed all humanity and all creation.

Our experience of receiving one another as gifts in our practice of conversation is quite rare among churches. Like infants who do not yet know that the parts of their body are connected and can be orchestrated to do wondrous things, many churches do not really know their members and the manifold gifts they each bring. Growing in our recognition and knowledge of one another was a gift of God's grace that rippled through every corner of our life together. This sort of recognition could not have been cultivated without our enduring commitment to hospitable conversation. Over time, these conversations formed us into a community that resembles the human body, consisting of many strikingly diverse members who recognize each other and the distinctive role each member plays—not only in the body's health, but in the sort of witness it bears to a fragmented and polarized world.

Hospitality guided us at Englewood Christian Church into the practice of conversation, and sustained us as we stumbled forward in this new practice. Conversation requires the mutuality of Christian hospitality, but it also transforms us into increasingly hospitable people. At Englewood in recent years, this hospitality has blossomed in a multitude of ways, including care for those who live in housing we own (as well as other neighbors), and participation with students and families of local public schools. The desire for diverse congregations that embody practices of hospitality and inclusion is not uncommon among churches today, but healthy embodiment of that diversity does not happen without intentional practice. Perhaps these desires may lead others churches into their own intentional practices of conversation.

Discussion Questions

1. How do you typically define and think of hospitality? Is there room for this conception to expand? How does Christian hospitality differ from cultural definitions of the concept?

2. Reflect on the most profound moments of hospitality you have experienced. Share those stories. What about those experiences reflected God's love and/or your belonging?

3. How does your church practice hospitality? Are these practices fruitful and effective?

4. Take some time to think about the individuals in your congregation. What needs or potential barriers to participation exist? (e.g. Do you have individuals with disabilities, who speak different languages, who need childcare, who need transportation?) What would be required for all community members to particulate fully in conversation?

Chapter Five

The Virtue of Dialogue (Or, Why Conversation is an Essential Practice of Church Communities)

[T]he kingdom of God is not in the wisdom of the world, nor in eloquence, but in the faith of the cross and in the virtue of dialogue.

— St. Cyprian

It might be tempting to dismiss our story as an aberration or similarly to say, "My church could never do that!" In this final chapter, I would like to sketch a brief outline of why I think conversation is an essential practice for all churches. Before I do so, however, let me emphasize that in saying I believe that conversation is an essential practice, I am *not* saying others churches should do exactly as we have done. Churches *should* find ways to carve out space in their life together for open and hospitable conversation that fits who and where they are.

In the wilderness, God led the ancient Israelite people in a cloud of fire; in the age of the church, God leads the people of God through dialogue in the church community that is grounded in the gifts of the Spirit. This gift of God's leadership is depicted throughout the Pauline epistles, but nowhere more clearly than in 1 Corinthians 12-14.[1]

If it is the Holy Spirit who unites us and gives particular gifts to each member of the church community (chapter 12), then as we gather together, we should make room for these gifts to interact with each other in a sort of conversation (14:26-40), and we must above all be sure that such conversation is guided by the love of Christ (chapter 13). In the last verses of chapter 14, Paul instructs the Corinthians that when they gather, everyone should come prepared to share out of the gifts given to each member. Paul explains that such dialogue, guided by the gifts of the Spirit, serves to drive the congregation toward maturity and one-mindedness. This passage also parallels Paul's description of the Holy Spirit's use of gifts to guide the Church toward maturity ("the fullness of Christ") in Ephesians 4, especially verses 11-13. Paul seems to assume a conversational life together in Ephesians 4 as well: note the place of dialogue (i.e., "speaking the truth in love") in verses 15 and 25.

Similarly, Acts 15 can be read as a case study in church dialogue. I encourage you to read this chapter, noting the place of debate (verse 7), its silencing (verse 12), and the tension between the perspectives of the believing Pharisees and that of Paul and Barnabas. The heart of this story, however, is the apostle James's summary—grounded in the unity of the gathering (verse 12)—that "it seemed good to the Holy Spirit and to us" (verses 25, 28). Having been given the "ministry of reconciliation" (2 Corinthians 5:17-20) exercised through the practice of congregational conversation, as described here, we began to see the assembly of our congregation, not as a form of selfish entertainment or vague religious duty, but as the place in which we imagine and discern the will of God together and are energized to undertake the fulfillment of God's redemptive purposes.

Congregational dialogue was a practice retained by early churches, even after the apostolic era. Throughout the first millennium of the church's history, the Council of Nicea and subsequent councils served to extend the practice of church dialogue beyond the local congregation, in hopes of uniting diverse churches across the broad span of the Roman Empire. Even during the turmoil of the Reformation, Luther and Zwingli both maintained a hope that their differences with the Roman Catholic Church could be resolved through convening a large-scale council of churches. Church communities, especially in the Anabaptist and Quaker traditions, continued to be formed by the practice of conversation well into the modern era.

So why has conversation become a lost practice in churches today? As I have shown, conversation is waning in the culture at large, but why does this cultural trend persist in churches?

Conversation is slow and often messy; it doesn't fit well with our industrialized culture that puts a premium on speed and efficiency. The shared life of most churches therefore typically takes a shape that minimizes conversation. One shortcut is our reliance on hierarchical and authoritarian forms of leadership in the local church; we appoint leaders to make decisions for the church as a way to avoid having to talk and make decisions together. Many of our churches find themselves within the hierarchical structures of a denomination, and I'm not saying that we should abolish those structures. Rather, with the leeway that we have in our local congregations for creating spaces for meaningful conversation, let us begin the process of learning how to make decisions in a non-hierarchical fashion there. I am hopeful that in learning to converse and make decisions faithfully together in our local church communities, we will eventually begin to see changes in the sorts of conversations that are possible in our broader relations with other churches.

In a similar vein, making decisions in the local church by voting is a way of avoiding conversation, particularly undercutting those who hold the minority position on any given issue. I do not intend to demonize voting here, but if we are going to make decisions democratically in our churches, we need to realize that some ways of voting promote conversation and other ways squelch conversation. Do we have spaces in which people can have meaningful discussion of an issue before it is voted on, or venues in which minority opinions can be heard and thoughtfully and prayerfully considered?

The size of our churches can also be a hindrance to conversation. Large congregations do not necessarily preclude conversation, but larger churches need smaller-sized groups in which conversation can occur. In many churches, small groups or cell groups can be a viable place for conversation to occur, although the life together that is shared in these groups needs to run deeper than simply a weekly Bible study. Anonymity and disengagement, both all too common in large churches, are antithetical to conversation, and in order to foster conversation, a larger church will need to find ways to connect people in smaller groups where meaningful conversation can occur.

Not all forms of conversation are beneficial. I would like to highlight two particular characteristics of healthy congregational conversation. First, our conversations must be Eucharistic, by which I mean not that they should be directly connected to our practice of this sacrament, but that we enter into conversation with the sort of radical self-denial that defined the life and death of Jesus and that we remember in the celebration of the Eucharist. It must be the Holy Spirit who speaks in our midst and guides our conversations. If we speak (or listen) out of our sinful nature, passions will be ignited and division will ensue. If we allow our selfish agendas to dominate our conversations (and particularly the "what's in it for me?" mentality), we are setting ourselves up for power struggles and many other kinds of trouble.

Thus, we at Englewood have found we experience the uniting power of the Spirit in our conversations and our life together only to the extent we have died to our selfish natures and are willing to let God speak and work through us. And in conversation, we are maturing together into the fullness of Christ's body, and we learn to deny the selfish desires of our hearts and to put others before ourselves, as Christ did. None of us are very good at following Christ in this way, but we certainly are not going to get any better by avoiding conversation and continuing in isolation. In real relationships and real conversation, we begin to see exactly how selfish we are, and as we continue in these conversations, God begins to slowly and gradually transform us.

Second, conversation should be open; anyone and everyone should be allowed to contribute. Open conversation in the church is rooted in the convictions that God has assembled us together in this place and that everyone God has assembled is a gift given for the maturing of Christ's body. Our conversations should be both Eucharistic and open; everyone should be permitted to speak, but those who speak should do so not out of self-promotion or selfish ambition. Silence and careful listening are just as important in church conversations as speaking. Sometimes we need to hear the particular wisdom of certain people (e.g., in reading and understanding a particular biblical text); at other times, it is just as necessary to hear the questions of one who does not understand something that has been said. One sister church is so committed to open conversation that they intersperse "pulse checks" in their conversation, in which they go around the room and encourage each person in turn to speak what's on their mind. "Pulse checks" may not work in every context, but they might be a helpful tool for some churches in the process of learning how to speak openly together.

Conversation is a hopeful practice; by discovering how to talk together in our churches, we are learning to be reconciled to each other. In a world that is rapidly losing the capacity for civil conversation, our churches need to create spaces in which we can talk together in open and Eucharistic ways. Our experience at Englewood has taught us that in learning to talk together within our church community, we become equipped to talk with our neighbors and others who are not in our church communities.

In nurturing public conversations that are open and focus more on the common good than on selfish desires, we participate in the healing, reconciling, and transforming work of Christ in our neighborhood. And it seems from reading scripture and church history that all churches are called into this flourishing life of conversation. As we seek to become a functioning body of Christ in which all members work and converse together, we come to realize the deep hope we have in Christ, a hope that is slowly and patiently transforming us through our conversations together.

The hope we realize in Christ is the hope of the world, the hope of the reconciliation of all people and all creation. Our job as congregations is to learn to talk together again and to allow our conversation to spill out of our churches and into our neighborhoods, a stream of hope scented with the rich fragrance of God's reconciliation, the shalom God desires for all creation.

May we abide faithfully in this calling!

Discussion Questions

1. Reflect on the structure and governance of your own congregation and/or denomination. In what ways does this structure promote or hinder Eucharistic, open conversation? Are there changes that need to be made?

2. If your congregation is to become one in which conversation plays a significant role, what changes might need to be made? What do you anticipate or hope the outcome of improved and elevated conversation be?

3. Spend some time reading 1 Corinthians 12-14 and Acts 15. What do these passages reveal about the practice of conversation?

4. In what ways can conversation be a reconciliatory practice? What are your hopes and desires for conversation within your own life and Christian communities?

---

1. Our congregation learned a great deal about congregational conversation in the early 2000s from John Howard Yoder's interpretation of this passage in Corinthians, and the following four paragraphs have been adapted from his chapters "The Fullness of Christ" and "The Rule of Paul" in *Body Politics: Five Practices of the Christian Community Before the Watching World* (Herald Press 2001). We did not realize at that time that Yoder was a sexual predator. Today, all of his work is appropriately being reassessed in light of his sexual sins. While it is doubtful that we would study his work today, this portion of his work did prove helpful to us in these early years of our conversational practices, as we tried to make sense of why it was important for us to talk together as a congregation.

Appendix A: Questions to Engage in Conversation

These questions guided our congregation as we considered, "Who are we called to be as a community of God's people?" (See Chapter 3 for more.)

1. According to the Bible, what is the ultimate end to which God is bringing all of creation? What is God doing in and with the world?

2. According to the Bible, how has God chosen to accomplish God's mission in the world? What is the role the Church has been given?

3. What are the particular strategic initiatives to which God has called Englewood Christian Church in participation with God's mission?

4. What is the place of our Covenant Agreements in Englewood's shared life? How have we used them in the past and how could we use them in the future?

5. What are our current practices for nurturing intentional congregational formation? What should we give more attention to or what should we change?

Appendix B: Our Conversational Norms

These "conversational norms" are a relatively new development in our practice of conversation at Englewood. They emerged from our conversations in the Spring of 2024 and still exist in a "trial" mode, with plans to discuss and finalize them in the near future. If your own congregation is beginning a conversation practice, it may prove worthwhile to spend some time determining together what guidelines would make your own conversations hospitable, fruitful, and beneficial to all.

- We listen and speak with an attitude which reflects the fruit of the Spirit.

- We reflect the promise of Christ's presence among us and in each one of us.

- We practice empathy.

- We seek to understand above being understood.

- We encourage openness and truthfulness by resisting judgement.

- We respect the participation of others by keeping our comments brief.

- We look for opportunities to find common ground.

- We resist being defensive.

- We are not afraid of silence.

- We always pursue reconciliation with one another.

- We expect messiness.

- We make every effort to come prepared and on time.

Works Consulted & Recommended Reading

To anyone interested in the rich history of the Englewood neighborhood, we recommend Brent Aldrich and C. Christopher Smith, *The Electric Glory of the Near Eastside: The Rollercoaster Ride of Englewood's Modern History* (Neighborhood Alliance Press, 2011).

Other books that have been helpful for us on our journey:

• Banks, Robert. *Paul's Idea of Community*. Grand Rapids: Baker, 1994.

• Berry, Wendell. "The Burden of the Gospels: An Unconfident Reader" in *The Christian Century*. 20 Sept. 2005.

• Berry, Wendell. "Two Economies" in *The Art of the Commonplace*. San Francisco: Counterpoint, 2003.

- Bishop, Bill. *The Big Sort: Why the Clustering of Like-Minded America is Tearing Us Apart*. New York: Mariner Books, 2008.

- Branson, Mark Lau. *Memories, Hopes, and Conversations: Appreciative Inquiry and Congregational Change*. Herndon, VA: Alban Institute, 2004.

- Brueggemann, Walter. *Journey to the Common Good*. Louisville: WJK Books, 2010.

- Brown, Juniata. *The World Café: Shaping Our Futures Through Conversations that Matter*. New York: Berrett-Koehler, 2005.

- Clapp, Rodney. *A Peculiar People: The Church as Culture in a Post-Christian Society*. Westmont, IL: IVP Books, 1996.

- Dark, David. *The Sacredness of Questioning Everything*. Grand Rapids: Zondervan, 2009.

- Dawn, Marva. *Joy in Divine Wisdom: Practices of Discernment from other Cultures and Christian Traditions*. San-Francisco: Jossey-Bass, 2006.

- Fowl, Stephen and Gregory Jones. *Reading in Communion*. Eugene, OR: Wipf and Stock, 1998.

- Hammond, Sue. *The Thin Book of Appreciative Inquiry (2nd Edition)*. Bend, OR: Thin Books, 1998.

- Hammond, Sue Annis and Andrea Mayfield. *The Thin Book of Naming Elephants: How to Surface Undiscussables for Greater Organizational Success*. Bend, OR: Thin Books, 2004.

- Johnson, Luke Timothy. *Scripture and Discernment: Decision-making in the Church*. Nashville: Abingdon, 1996.

- Kenneson, Philip. *Life on the Vine: Cultivating the Fruit of the Spirit in Christian Community*. Westmont, IL: IVP Books, 2003.

- Lohfink, Gerhard. *Does God Need The Church? Toward a Theology of the People of God*. Collegeville, MN: Michael Glazier Books, 1999.

- Palmer, Parker. *To Know As We Are Known: Education as A Spiritual Journey*. San Francisco: HarperOne, 1993.

- Putnam, Robert. *Bowling Alone: The Collapse and Revival of American Community*. New York: Simon and

Schuster, 2001. • Wilson-Hartgrove, Jonathan. *The Wisdom of Stability*. Brewster, MA: Paraclete Press, 2011.

• Yoder, John Howard. *Body Politics: Five Practices of the Christian Community Before the Watching World*. Scottdale, PA: Herald Press 2001. (See cautionary footnote in Chapter 5 about Yoder's work.)

About the Author

C. Christopher Smith is a member of the Englewood Christian Church community and editor of *The Englewood Review of Books*. He and his wife Jeni have three adult children and live in a house across the parking lot from the Englewood church building, which they have shared with a number of church members over the years. In addition to editing *The Englewood Review of Books,* Chris is the author of numerous books, including the award-winning *Slow Church* (2014, co-authored with John Pattison) and his most recent, *How the Body of Christ Talks: Recovering the Practice of Conversation in the Church* (2019). All of his work—reading, writing, speaking—focuses on helping congregations cultivate a deeper life together by reading, thinking, imagining, and most importantly, by talking together. He regularly teaches these interwoven practices in congregational, academic, denominational, and ecumenical settings.

Also by C. Christopher Smith:

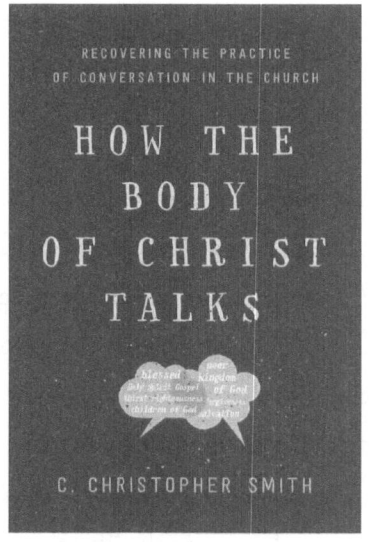

For more on the theological foundations of conversation and stories about how other congregations practice this discipline, read How the Body of Christ Talks: Recovering the Practice of Conversation in the Church.

Thanks for reading!

If you enjoyed this book, please leave a review at Amazon or your favorite online retailer.

Englewood Press is partnership between Cultivating Communities and *The Englewood Review of Books.*

Connect with *The Englewood Review of Books:*

englewoodreview.org
facebook.com/erbks
instagram.com/erbooks
bsky.app/profile/erbks.bsky.social

www.ingramcontent.com/pod-product-compliance
Lightning Source LLC
Chambersburg PA
CBHW060537080526
44586CB00012B/770